Cuckoo's Blood

Also by Stephen Berg

ANTHOLOGIES

Naked Poetry (with Robert Mezey)
Between People (with S.J. Marks and J. Michael Pilz)
About Women (with S.J. Marks)
In Praise of What Persists
Singular Voices
The Body Electric (with David Bonanno and Arthur Vogelsang)
My Business Is Circumference: On Influence and Mastery

Cuckoo's Blood

Versions of Zen Masters

Stephen Berg

foreword by Steven Antinoff

COPPER CANYON PRESS
PORT TOWNSEND, WASHINGTON

Dōgen

Bashō

Crazy Cloud Ikkyū

Daito

Hui-neng

Issa

Seng ts'an

Han-shu

Joshu

Buson

Shen-hui

Ta-hui

Feng-kuan

Bankei

Ryōkan

Hakuin

Printed in the United States of America

Cover art: Brice Marden, *Vine*, 1991–1993. Oil on linen,
96 x 102 inches. Courtesy of the artist.

A few of these poems first appeared in *The Steel Cricket: Versions
1958–1997* and were hand printed by Harry Duncan.

Copper Canyon Press is in residence at Fort Worden State Park in
Port Townsend, Washington, under the auspices of Centrum. Centrum
is a gathering place for artists and creative thinkers from around the
world, students of all ages and backgrounds, and audiences seeking
extraordinary cultural enrichment.

LIBRARY OF CONGRESS CATALOGING-IN-PUBLICATION DATA
Berg, Stephen.
  Cuckoo's blood : versions of Zen masters / Stephen Berg.
    p. cm.
  ISBN 978-1-55659-268-3 (pbk. : alk. paper)
  I. Title.

PS3552.E7C83 2008
811'.54—dc22

2007040092

98765432 FIRST PRINTING

COPPER CANYON PRESS
Post Office Box 271
Port Townsend, Washington 98368
www.coppercanyonpress.org

In memory of Eric Sackheim

...but my life itself couldn't very conceivably be less Zenful than it is, and what little I've been able to apprehend—I pick that verb with care—of the Zen experience has been a by-result of following my own rather natural path of extreme Zenlessness.

Buddy Glass, from *Seymour: An Introduction,* by J.D. Salinger

It's hard to see what you're seeing with, to see what being is as an activity through the instrument of whatever-it-is we have being in.

Robert Hass, from "Conciousness," *Time and Materials: Poems 1997–2005*

Contents

Foreword

Zen Art versus Zen Quest Art

I. ZEN ART VERSUS ZEN QUEST ART

The Zen monk Bunko Kiku used to meditate in the monastery's bell tower or in the cubbyhole by the kitchen, which was behind my tiny room, to avoid being ribbed for his zealousness by the less-motivated monks. The last time I saw him, twenty-five years later in the village temple where he now lives alone, he picked up a ballpoint pen, drew one side of a mountain from base to summit, and said, "Meditation takes you to *here.*

"But Zen," he added, drawing a descending line from summit to base to form the far side of the mountain, "is the movement to *here.*"

Shin'ichi Hisamatsu (1889–1980), Zen master and professor of aesthetics, defined the aesthetic dimension of this in an obscure colloquium held in Germany in 1958, whose participants included Martin Heidegger:

> In Zen art, skill means two things: through skill man is led from reality to the source of reality; art is the way by which man can enter the source. On the other hand, art is the way by which man, having entered the source, "returns" to reality. The essence of Zen art lies in this return. This return is the activity of Zen. Zen truth itself lies in this activity, and in it resides the significance of Zen works of art. The above-mentioned source of reality is the original true life or self. It is the separation from all bonds, the release from the fetters intrinsic to all form. This

release is also called nothingness. All these terms
mean the same thing... The essence of Zen lies not in
going toward the source but returning from it.[1]

Hisamatsu might disagree, but I think he points not simply
to two kinds of art, one religious and one not—but to two
kinds of religious art: art that seeks the source of reality and art
that seeks to express that source once it is attained. These
two—"art toward" and "art from"—may be distinguished as
"Zen quest (or, broadly speaking, 'religious quest') art" and
"Zen art."

That "art toward" can be as religious as "art from"—and
even aesthetically superior—may be clearer in the light of Paul
Tillich's famous definition of religion as "the state of being
grasped by an ultimate concern." One's ultimate concern is that
which concerns one unconditionally whatever the specific con-
ditions of one's existence, such as race, gender, personal psy-
chology, or the era or culture in which one lives. Under this
definition it is obvious—and here Tillich was insistent—that an
artist with zero interest in any specific religion, religious
doctrine, religious organization or affiliation, may be far more
religious than the priest. Hisamatsu concurs: "The so-called
religious person in the ordinary sense... does not reach the feet
of a literary figure such as Dostoyevsky. There are occasions
when the man of letters, rather than the man of religion and his
writings, educates us to the truth of the human situation."[2]

"'Art toward' as the existential struggle to enter the source
of reality" takes on the structure and function of a koan. This

---

1. Alcopley (Alfred L. Copley), *Listening to Heidegger and Hisamatsu* (Kyoto: Bokubi
Press, 1963), 54. Translation modified. For the Japanese text see ibid., 52, 58.
Published in a limited edition of 800 copies, the book includes—together with
drawings by Alcopley—German, English, and Japanese transcriptions of the collo-
quium in which Hisamatsu, Heidegger, Alcopley, and others participated. The book
has long been out of print.

2. Shin'ichi Hisamatsu, "Hontô no Jiko ni Mezameru" [Awakening to the True Self],
in *Hisamatsu Shin'ichi Chosaku-shû* [The Collected Works of Shin'ichi Hisamatsu]
(Tokyo: Risô-sha, 1969–1980), 2:39–40.

may be understood by examining the structural parallel between what Hisamatsu called the *fundamental koan*—"When whatever you do will not do, what do you do?"—and what Samuel Beckett set out as the mandate for future artistic expression: "The expression that there is nothing to express, nothing with which to express, nothing from which to express, no power to express, no desire to express, together with the obligation to express."[3] Both formulations pose the contradiction inherent in any true koan: absolute negation and absolute demand. *Absolute negation* in that until "art toward" is "art from" it cannot attain its aim. So long as it is "toward" the source it has not "entered"—the artwork is repulsed by angels with flaming swords, and even if the artwork is not repulsed, the artist is. Yet the art koan always sets forth simultaneously an *absolute demand*. The Zen quest artist, or any artist in the grip of an ultimate concern, cannot cease striving to arrive at the source, even though infinitely thwarted.

2. "ART TOWARD"

"The essential in Zen art," says Hisamatsu, "is not to gain and possess the source but to let the source appear."[4] Art *toward* the source of reality may let the source appear through some momentary experience of the Ultimate that thereafter eludes the artist, who can only speak of it from a standpoint of exclusion, as does a drunken Edmund in Eugene O'Neill's *Long Day's Journey into Night:*

> for a moment I lost myself—actually lost my life. I
> was set free! I dissolved in the sea, became white
> sails and flying spray, became beauty and rhythm,

3. Samuel Beckett and George Duthuit, "Three Dialogues," in *Art in Theory: 1900–1990,* ed. Charles Harrison and Paul Wood (Oxford: Blackwell Publishers Ltd., 1992), 606.

4. Alcopley, *Listening to Heidegger and Hisamatsu,* 54.

became moonlight and the ship and the high dim-starred sky! I belonged, without past or future, within peace and unity and a wild joy, within something greater than my own life, or the life of Man, to Life itself! To God, if you want to put it that way... Like a saint's vision of beatitude. Like the veil of things as they seem drawn back by an unseen hand. For a second you see—and seeing the secret, are the secret. For a second there is meaning! Then the hand lets the veil fall and you are alone, lost in the fog again, and you stumble on toward nowhere, for no good reason![5]

The source may appear through an intrinsic blindness, as in Rilke's Eighth Elegy, where humans are eternally closed off from "the Open," the non-objectifiable Infinity, which human awareness, twisting away from its source, can apprehend only as an inaccessible, longed-for object of consciousness.

Never, not for a single day do *we* have
before us that pure space into which flowers
endlessly open. Always there is World
and never Nowhere without the [negating] No.
. . . .
Forever turned toward objects, we see in them
the mere reflection of the realm of freedom,
which we have dimmed.

. . . .
That is what fate means: to be opposite,
to be opposite and nothing else, forever.

. . . .

---

5. This passage in act 4 was brought to my attention by Dr. Joanna Rotté of the theater department of Villanova University.

Who has twisted us around like this, so that
no matter what we do, we are in the posture
of someone going away?[6]

The source may be made visible as an ever-present reality
that we cannot separate from but, paradoxically, have no access
to, so that our inseparability is profitless. For Stephen Berg,
the source appears as a *must* that cannot be made to appear,
bisected by a quest to make it appear that can be neither toler-
ated nor relinquished.

3. THE POET AS KOAN

Berg writes torn by the contradiction between life and art that
consistently negates him and his demand for release.

He cannot—and must—transcend, and tries not to want to
transcend, though his *trying not to want* is because he cannot.
Berg is the last person to consider himself even remotely in the
grip of a spiritual concern: "art toward," in his case, far from a
conscious striving, is a Lieutenant Columbo–like stumbling for
a way out of his discomfort. As Kafka would have it: "The true
way leads along a tight-rope, which is not stretched aloft but
just above the ground. It seems more designed to trip one than
to be walked along."[7] Berg's quest is a falling on his face, but
where he hits the ground hardest the cement holds something
ultimate.

In his recent book $X=$ Berg is filed down to the bald polari-
ties of his contradiction.[8] The opening poem already exposes
the religious dimension of his predicament.

he says all activity is prayer bullshit (3)

---

6. Ranier Maria Rilke, *The Selected Poetry of Ranier Maria Rilke,* ed. and trans.
   Stephen Mitchell (New York: Vintage International, 1989), 193, 197.

7. Franz Kafka, "The Collected Aphorisms," in *The Great Wall of China and
   Other Short Works,* ed. and trans. Malcolm Paisley, (London: Penguin Books,
   1991), 79.

8. Stephen Berg, $X=$ (Urbana: University of Illinois Press, 2002).

It is a frightening line; the words of a man who would so much like to lie to himself about the value of his acts, to infuse them with a power to save he desperately needs them to have, but whose honesty rejects his attempts to do so. This first poem, "Biker," begins with a double entendre,

he gets on

he gets off he gets on (1)

that immediately opens out into the world of Vladimir struggling daily with Estragon's boot, and with almost identical significance. For just as the never-to-end efforts to get the boot off or on are infested, as is all else in *Waiting for Godot*, with Beckett's opening sentence, "Nothing to be done," so Berg's simple acts of mounting, dismounting, remounting his bicycle are a trap sprung on the author even before the bike is wheeled out of the house. He gets on (with life, somehow); occasionally he gets off (as in the phone sex in the poem "Phonefun," or in the rare releases from his human entrapment), but the getting off—transient—invariably subsides into the default mode of a getting on that is a mix of crazed perseverance and a bare getting through the days.

The deceptively nonpoetic form of the book reflects this predicament. With the exception of one poem, virtually every line in *X=* begins with the word *he*. For the first third of the book most lines don't run the width of the page. The poems read like a list. He (Berg) does or thinks this; in the next line he thinks or feels that. In one sense the sequence of lines does not matter, and it is this that makes the list so horrible. The formal simplicity asks for the book to be read in a radical way as yet beyond human capacity. Not sentence by sentence, with each line taking up its sequence in time, but all lines read simultaneously, since the dilemma in any one line inheres in all: "he felt the truth the crime whose punishment was the simple undeniable fact of one's life as it is" (18).

And how is "one's life as it is"? It is life unable to eat from the Tree of Life. Life somehow drained of life when it ought to be overflowing with it; life unable to accept its barrenness, nor able to turn activity into the prayer it must be if barrenness is to be overcome. Stephen Berg torn on this schism is the "ontological proof" of the original sin that cannot be done away with even when God is done away with. A split down the length of him precedes, and accompanies, all he does, thwarting his being even prior to his act, and against which his acts are an effort to contend. It is critical to his self-understanding that the schism is composed of not just barrenness, or self-conflict, but equally of the desperate need for transcendence. In this Berg truly is the brother of Kafka, who wrote in his diary of 1920, also titled, by strange coincidence, *"He"*: "He has the feeling that merely by being alive he is blocking his own way." "His own frontal bone blocks his way (he bloodies his brow by beating against his own brow)." "He has discovered the Archimedean principle, but he has turned it to account against himself; evidently it was only on this condition that he was permitted to discover it."[9]

Berg is all this against his will, as every "I" is "I" against its will, as consciousness comes to us against our will, though no one other than "I" can will it:

> he was in the present but did not want to be because
> here consciousness is this is who he is his mind
> not what he wants it to be the wrong mind insol-
> uble for too long he would have torn it out like a
> dead bush but it continued... (30)

Line after line he attempts an assault on his insoluble mind. He tries through learning:

---

9. Kafka, "The Collected Aphorisms" in *The Great Wall of China and Other Short Works*, 105, 106.

he will read another hundred books ransacking pages
he will underline and scrawl arrows in the margins
he will write exclamation points beside brilliant
    remarks and drop them down into the savage
    clutter of his need... (7)

And ends fed up with the "fraud of serious words" (18), "tired
of the bullshit profundities of clear description and brilliant
thought" (10), skewered on the one brilliant thought he cannot
dismiss as bullshit, Paul Tillich's:

> [I]ntellectual endeavor can as little attain the ultimate
> truth as moral endeavor can attain the ultimate good.
> He who attempts it deepens the estrangement.[10]

He tries through writing and ends "disgusted with poetry
the word the thing" (10), no more able to stop writing than
reading, and no less ambivalent: "he believed writing would
accomplish it he believed writing wouldn't be worth shit" (45).

He proposes to himself a life of heroic compassion that he
knows is a joke since he has seen himself incapable of it beyond
sporadic surges of pity. "I could give away every cent table
chair shirt... slash my wrists in homage to Rwandan suffering...
I'd rather get my cock sucked on the phone by a high school
girlfriend who always loved to do it that way" (36–37).

He longs to annul human consciousness: to be a bird, a
rat, a tree, a dog: "he sees a dog as the self he'll never be so
deeply taken care of by the universe by life itself" (31). And
always, always he longs, in the midst of all other attempts and
longings, for that same unity, not through annulment, but
through the breaking beyond the mitosis of consciousness that
divides him against himself in every aspect of his being. The
result is a new suit for the old split: the unity that he can't live

---

10. Paul Tillich, *Biblical Religion and the Search for Ultimate Reality* (Chicago:
    The University of Chicago Press, 1955), 55.

without is exactly what he is not; Berg is addicted to an ulti-
mate he cannot believe, deny, or attain:

> he has even forced himself for days to work on problems
>   like eternity immortality faith salvation terms the
>   mind sets up like gaudy rockets to distract us
> he has wanted to smash himself against those words like
>   a brick hurled through a window
> he has spoiled ordinary days
> he has haunted their vicinity like a starved dog
> he has crippled himself with oneness and being (11)

> he had read so much Zen it was coming out his ears did
>   nothing ruined his common sense confused irritated
>   infuriated
> he knew he had gone to it because of pain bought all the
>   books underlined arrowed starred bracketed
>   memorized forgot picked out passages that struck a
>   chord flotsam and jetsam of salvation
> he knew he was trying to ward off life the whole
>   enlightenment shtick sucked him in he sat half-closed
>   his eyes let thoughts float in out across down up
> he even believed for very brief moments that it had
>   happened he was there he knew what he knew in a
>   deep way but then immediately he would be who he
>   was again the same old stupid ordinary Steve (32)

In the end Stephen Berg is where he begins; negated
whether he gets on or gets off, he abandons the ride. He sits at
the computer. He types.

That act, like every human act that wishes to be ultimate,
regenerates the ineradicable question of whether negation or
affirmation is to have the last word. Berg's answer is, of course,
ambiguous. The words he types are subverted the instant they

emerge on the screen—an incoherent dying dictation from Henry James that ends with the enigmatic sentence: "Problems are very sordid."

"Of course, ambiguous"—or more precisely, ambivalent—must therefore mark Stephen Berg's decades-long relationship to Zen and to Zen poetry. In the twenty years I have known him he has always been skeptical of the "awakening" of the Zen figures whom he has revered. The words once uttered by his beloved Sung dynasty master Ta-hui are his: "My position is that of a dog which stands by a fat-boiling pot: he cannot lick it however badly he wants to, nor can he go away from it though he may wish to quit."[11] Hisamatsu writes: "Whether we know it or not we cannot stop searching for the ultimate."[12] In Hisamatsu's fundamental koan—"When whatever you do will not do, what do you do?"—the "will not do" likewise will not do. For that reason no one gives up the quest even if he or she tries to put it aside. It is within that contradiction that Berg works out his renditions of Zen poetry. He can, in the koan of Chao Chou, neither drop it nor carry it away.

In a letter to me after the completion of the book now before the reader, Berg writes:

> the only emotion i feel now after 50 years—hammering at it in my indolent way—in response to the versions is grief in the realization of the huge distance there is between me and some entrance into that world, a world i should never have imagined would work for me—no big deal—the truth.

I see Berg's engagement with the poets in this volume not so much as an attempt to realize Zen as a fighting his way free of

11. Quoted in Daisetz Teitaro Suzuki, *Essays in Zen Buddhism: Second Series* (New Delhi: Munshiram Manoharlal Publishers Pvt. Ltd., 2000), 30.

10. Shin'ichi Hisamatsu, "After My Student Life," *F.A.S. Society Journal* (Winter 1985–86), 1, trans. Gishin Tokiwa. See Shin'ichi Hisamatsu, "Gakkyû Seikatsu Igo [After My Student Life]," 1:435, for the Japanese text.

it, aware that he cannot succeed, that if he did succeed he would be diminishing what is fundamental in himself.

4. "ART FROM"

Zen art is the art created by the Self that has broken beyond the duality between being and nonbeing. To do so is, for Zen, to enter the source of reality, which Hisamatsu calls *Zettai Mu*, or Absolute Nothingness, but which he also calls *Zettai Sonzai to Zettai Kachi*—Absolute Existence and Absolute Value. There can be bad Zen art. As Richard DeMartino used to say: "Just because you're Jesus Christ doesn't mean you can play the violin."

Zen holds there is an artistry that precedes artistic expression through an art medium. D.T. Suzuki called those capable of such artistry the "artists of life." Hisamatsu is more specific: There is Zen art (as expressed in the various media such as painting, pottery, theater, music, and dance). There is the artistry that precedes Zen art—these are the everyday gestures of the awakened Self. And there is the artistry that precedes even these gestures:

> When in the raising of a hand or in a single step something of Zen is present, that Zen content seems to me to possess a very specific, artistic quality. A narrow conception of art might not accept that such manifestations contain anything artistic, but it seems to me that they possess an artistic quality that ordinarily cannot be seen. In fact, in such vital workings of Zen, I believe that something artistic but also beyond art is involved, something toward which art should aim at as its goal.
>
> Besides this concrete, manifestative aspect, however, Zen also has an aspect that is "prior to form." For example, when a worthy monk is neither speaking nor moving but just sitting silently before us, there will be

something about him that cannot be judged by our usual understanding of silence or quietude, something that is more than either talk or silence, movement or stillness, in their ordinary meanings. We can think of this quality as also being artistic.

This "prior to form" quality is far more basic than the concrete expressions of Zen Activity, for only with the presence of the former is the Activity given meaning. This quality is spoken of in Zen as "when not one thing is brought forth," "where not one particle of dust is raised," "prior to the separation of heaven and earth," "utterance before voice," "not one word spoken," and so on.

Fundamentally, I feel that here something differs from ordinary art, something that art can only attain by transcending itself. From the Zen point of view, this "prior to form" phenomenon is the most basic art. It comes into being at the moment in which Zen is truly present. Compared with this, Zen dialogues, the use of various utensils, or the perception of aspects of nature... are derivative in the sense that such manifestations are infused with meaning by the "prior to form" quality.[13]

What an intriguing statement—that the perception of nature, so basic to Zen aesthetics, is secondary and derivative! Yet just as the ultimate concern of Zen, as is said in the Nineteenth Case of *The Blue Cliff Record,* is where to fix the eye before a single flower blooms, the ultimate concern of Zen poetry is to utter the "utterance before voice." In a 1957 conversation with Harvard psychologist Jerome Bruner, Hisamatsu made the identical point in terms of music:

---

13. Shin'ichi Hisamatsu, *Zen and the Fine Arts,* trans. Gishin Tokiwa (Tokyo: Kodansha International Ltd., 1971), 12–13.

I went to a concert yesterday, the Boston Symphony, with music by Beethoven and Schubert and others. It was lovely music but it stayed within the limits of sound, within its own medium. It does not break into the bottom of the world of sound, does not break through it. Truly great music would be music which negated sound, the paradox of sound negating sound. That is deep music.[14]

In his postscript to the published transcript of this conversation, Hisamatsu adds:

Western music is based on sound. The music of Noh (yokyoku) has as its basis no-sound, soundlessness, or one may say "Great Silence"... Great Silence is nothing but True Self, Formless Self. The music of Noh comes from that basis. Western music expresses sound, but characteristic Eastern music such as Noh expresses the soundless with sound. Here the sound is the expression of the activity of the soundless... The Noh music reverberates True Self, bottomless self. Viewed from the reversed side, it is felt as expressions of Bottomless Self.[15]

Consider Bashō's:

The temple bell has ceased
but the sound continues in the flowers.

Or an anonymous verse cited by Hisamatsu:

A bird cries. The mountain quiet deepens.
An ax rings out. Mountain stillness grows.

---

14. Jerome Bruner, "The Art of Ambiguity: A Conversation with Zen Master Hisamatsu," *Psychologia* 2, no. 2 (1959): 104. *Psychologia* was a quarterly journal, now defunct, published in Kyoto.

15. Ibid., 106.

In these verses Great Silence, literally, is the Subject, audible because of the crow's caw or the ax hacking the tree. Hisamatsu writes:

> A verse reading "not a bird cries. The mountain is very quiet" would be bereft of life, indicating nothing more than a naive and shallow quiet. The quiet that appears from the bird's cry is qualitatively different from that where no cry is heard. It possesses at its base a limitlessness of expression, while the latter is nothing but a monotonous and simple absence. Only with the quietude and depth that forms the basis of this source, what I call the Fundamental Subject that is Dynamic Nothingness, is true profundity or Profound Subtlety possible.[16]

What he describes as "the paradox of sound negating sound" has parallels in all Zen arts—the paradox of "stillness in motion, motion in stillness" in dance, for example. The greatest Noh dancers are unmoved-movers. Yet as Masao Abe liked to say, "stillness in motion, motion in stillness" is at the root of all Zen culture.[17] Stillness here is not the dualistic opposite of motion but what Hisamatsu called Absolute Nothingness or Great Silence disclosed in some movement, as in these poems of Dōgen:

Snowy heron
on the snowfield
hides itself
by being itself
invisible winter grass

---

16. Hisamatsu, *Zen and the Fine Arts*, 88.

17. In Japanese: *dô chû sei nari sei chû dô nari.*

Geese
leaving arriving
disappear
not a trace
and always know
where they are

I can't be seen in the gushing stream not
even there

Or Ikkyū's:

wind howls like a wolf goes silent
not one wolf has ever been seen in this district

Or Daito's:

through form through sound
in either place
you can't see me
so many years begging

Chuang Tzu names this "hiding the universe in the uni-verse." For Zen, the ultimate artistry is to actualize oneself as the nonduality of "is" and "is not"—what Hisamatsu calls the Self without life-and-death playing freely through its living and dying. To awaken to the Self without life-and-death in the midst of life-and-death is to enter the source of reality. One can only enter the source *as* the source; so long as they are two, the source does not exist. As the source (Great Silence, Great Stillness, Absolute Nothingness), one moves it when one moves. I love how D.T. Suzuki puts it: the walker must be the Way. The pen, the voice, the leap are then the source in movement. That is what my monk friend meant in completing his mountain.

Steven Antinoff

Preface

Cuckoo's Blood is mostly a collection of free versions based on
several translators' English translations. Over a period of about
fifty years, in the process of composition, I also wrote a few
poems that are completely my own. Why did these texts attract
me? I suppose I thought they might help me in ways I can't
name; my habit of rewriting translations drove me. I realized
recently that the first book I read on so-called Zen—bought
fifty-five years ago—was Hubert Benoit's *The Supreme
Doctrine*. I have no idea why I picked it out. Maybe the title
intrigued me. Since then I have read everything I could lay my
hands on about this unnameable experience, this "man of no
rank" vision. Not one word in any of those books, including
this one, can give me what I need.

SB

Cuckoo's Blood

Like That

Buddha

I came to crush time to study you to teach
Like a cloud drifting above you I darken everything I hide the
    sky
Crowned with lightning I save you with rain
Exactly like that like a raincloud I rise and point the way
Soothe your withered body know your pain ease it
Truth is the same for everyone—no hatred no love
Equal to all moral immoral I awaken all
When I rain down Truth you use it each in his way you live
    again
Shrubs grass bushes delicate plants huge trees
And the human world blossoms exactly like that
You I life death squeezed into a raindrop

Dōgen

1

Ignorant self
I'll never be a Buddha but
let this monk
bring you across

Asleep awake
in a grass hut
I'll do anything
to get you there first

Fantastic!
just studying old words
of all the Buddhas
to get beyond it

I'm afraid to stop
by the little brook
in the valley
because maybe my shadow will
flow into the world

Snowy heron
on the snowfield
hides itself
by being itself
invisible winter grass

Windy spring
peach blossoms
torn away
doubts don't grow
branches and leaves

Geese
leaving arriving
disappear
not a trace
and always know
where they are

Waves receding
wind doesn't anchor
a flimsy empty boat moon
a clear sign of midnight

Night sitting hour after hour no sleep yet
trees on the mountain needed for the way
brook in my ears moonlight in my eyes
nothing else not a shred of thought

I clean the moon with my robe I plow the clouds
Zen came from the west I moved it east
worldly red dusts blowing here?
night now deep in the hills inside my hut

Big cold skycolored lake
night quiet a sequined fish on the bottom swims
this way and that arrow notch split
surface brilliant with moonlight

False real tangled my whole damned life
mocking wind toying with the wind listening to birds
years wasted looking at the snowcovered mountain
this winter I realize suddenly snow makes a mountain

In the old days at Shaolin the same snowdrifts
sky earth spring all new
robe inherited sucking marrow joining the ancients
how could you pass up standing all night in the snow

Mind's the whole thing
practice is hard easy to explain
not-mind not-Buddha
to explain's hard practice is easy

Infinite world waxing waning
who gets here and understands undeluded?
iron ox blocks the Milky Way
at the peak a nameless dog at your heels

Where the hub revolves the sky is moving
pierce it no trace on thread road
alone on my balcony I sing moonwhite clouds
winter drizzle fiery haze

Inside sunface eye moonface
mastering sutra blinds you eye's the sutra
study mastery finally nothing outside
cloud blue sky water jar

Koan like a hot coal sixteen nights long
bodymoon tries to be full mindmoon fades
clear idea of moon moon will be born
hold the mid-autumn moon in your hand

Speech silence the same subtle profound
good cure prescribed eons ago
piercing sky embracing earth endless
one mammoth escarpment glowing with strange light

Shout bursts out and cracks the empty sky
clear immediate self-understanding
swallow down past Buddhas ancestors
follow nobody realize complete penetration

Nonthinking nothing is here complete
moving with nonthinking
immediately it appears
not here complete
completeness is to realize
if it appears right now now
nothing stains it
when completeness is realization
you're not caught in the general the particular
immediacy with stain
immediacy's "dropping away" nothing in your way

realize no general no particular
effort but no desire
clear water to the bottom
fish swims like a fish
sky utterly loved
bird flies like a bird

Everything you see's caused by your intimate depths
walking sitting lying body's complete truth
if you ask the inner meaning of this
it's a single grain of dust in the dharma eye

No doubt nothing's sacred hard as iron
tested in a furnace melts like snow
listen where does it go?
high breakers what's the moon look like?

Fifty-five years light up the sky
trembling leap smash a billion worlds
my whole body looking for nothing
living plunging

Icicles

frail grassblade walking the road to Kyoto lost
among mists on Kinobe Pass

I ache for the moon over Kyoto one last time deeper than ever
    this
autumn night can't sleep stung by its beauty

dayandnight nightandday everyday life the sutra
sings in each act in our hearts

monkeys' mystical screech peak after peak valleys below
sutra music being preached

your heart sutra's heart same heart admit it even the raucous
marketplace is what it is

brown gouges green patches on the hills valley streams move
    together
like Buddha's bodyvoice

amazing a graceful horse galloping past the rush of sunlight few
    know
this blur is the way

first snow more than a foot deep 1,224 September red leaves
    laden with
it impossible not to sing about it

an oyster washed up onto a high cliff waves battering the rocky
    coast
reach it but it stays right there

nobody's anyone he's the true man infinite wild blue
sky everyone everywhere

peach petals opening the spring breeze killing all doubts
　　　distracted
by leaves and branches

geese leave no trace landing taking off the paths they follow in
　　　their blood

no words it's always being uttered words can't show you what
　　　it's like
never fully say it

the scarecrow looks harmless on the hillside above the rice
　　　paddy
but it's far from useless

midnight moonglow frames the flimsy drifting boat
no waves no breezes

the flowers I'm talking about never die spring winter
their reds yellows pinks forever bright

awake asleep in my grass hut I pray compassion
permeates the world

let this idiot priest be the raft to carry you
across

four horses of suffering four steeds of compassion
how can you wake unless you ride them?

peaks valleys darkening cicada louder louder at twilight
grieving over the lost day

deluded whichever way I turn my futile mind stumbles over
its own deceptive self-deceptions

night long as the long sleek tail of the pheasant
dawn breaks through

finally they're my companions again—my father's face oh
and my mother's!

even for the humble poor spring bursts through the gates
time to pluck young herbs thriving in the fields

clear moon mind empty as the open sky ravish me lost
in the shadows it throws down

words I guess the primordial words
of innumerable Buddhas ceaselessly heard wherever I go

all last night and this morning snow blocks the deepest mountains
no autumn leaves on the floor of my house

white clouds swathing the frosted peaks slopes
trapped in my hut

the only prayer I know now awake asleep is to
save others before myself

idle as a dry leaf could sit here forever seeking
"the way" vanished like smoke

no ear no sound nothing interferes no voice no
speaker

icicle hanging from a mosquito net
is Buddha

world's an elephant's tail that won't go through the window
nobody's holding it back

plants trees heartless wither with the days knowing this
how can I live?

do they realize I can't hold back my tears when the sun sets
the valley streams high peaks?

moon mind free of everything even the ragged waves crashing
        sparkle
with its light

because my mind is free when I hear rain dripping from the
        eaves
who am I but the rain

white heron invisible in the snowy field green winter grass
also unseen

lightning bug's soft light pulses against the faint mountain
        ridge
gray moon

say this world is like the moon shining in dewdrops shaken
from a crane's bill

I can't be seen in the gushing stream not
even there

moon so far beyond the peak isn't my friend on this hill it
        can't
disappear it must come back to light this passing world

fifty-five years working at it now death crushes every obstacle
        and me
unbelievable to have nothing still alive plunged into endless
        fire

Bashō

Fishbones

Banana leaves tick
rain drips into a bucket
tick tick

Clouds will rip
my friend from me
after the wild geese flee

High wind dead tea leaves
thrash the brushwood gate
hail crashes down

I'm still like that old old oak
if I cupped November frost in my hand
hot tears would melt it

Another year I walk
hat on my head
sandals on my feet

Start the fire
I'll show you
a nice big snowball

So many things
have happened
those cherry blossoms!

Rough sea stretching toward
Sado Island
billions of stars

Cuckoo moonlight
seeps through
the lush bamboo

Monkey mask
on the monkey's face
year after year

Morning glory twined
iron bolt locks
the front yard gate

This autumn
why am I ill?
a bird reaches the clouds

On the road nauseated
my dreams hover
above the withered field

Night's delicate eyelids close
on pines and silent hills
my body dark as the darkness

You? me? dream?
I can't recall
real? asleep? awake?

Cold wind wails
through the open sliding door
pierces me

In this crazy world
snow shrouds
the bamboo thicket

Waves on blue sea
rice wine wafts in
brightening the moon

I cut down a tree
amazed by the fresh raw
moonlit stump

Spider sing
to me
in the biting wind

I humbly believe hell's
like this
autumn evening

Quietly under the moon
a worm gnaws
through a chestnut

A monk comes back
holding an umbrella
where did it rain?

Crow on a bare
branch
gray gray gray

Oars beating
the night waves
chill my bowels

I weep ice bitter
in a thirsty
sewer rat's mouth

An inch of whitefish
whiteness
in the sallow dawn

Last night of March
ancient cedars
tortured by a storm

Bucket of azaleas
a woman shreds dried codfish
close to their petals

Orchid odor
breathed
into butterfly wings

Wind gusting ice
through bamboo
calm shadowy sea

A wild duck's
shriek is
faintly white

Blooming by the roadside
rose mallow
gobbled by a horse

On the mountain road
heartbreaking
wild violet

Lone butterfly shadow
crossing
the sunlit field

So bleak
cricket hanging
from a nail

Cricket chanting
its shrill cry
into rocks

A frog hops into
the scummy pond
without knowing it

On this icy night
a water jar
splits open

My frozen shadow
leeks piled washed white
a minute ago

It's freezing!
hail splatters harshly
on my straw hat

First snow
daffodil leaves
bent by it

Shriveled chrysanthemum buds
right on time give off a sweet scent
after heavy rain

Chimes
fading fragrance of cherry
continues in the dust

One or two inches
above dry grass
heat waves shimmer

And shimmer
on the shoulders
of my paper robe

Monk sipping
his morning tea
serene chrysanthemums

I clap for dawn
and the summer moon
echoes it

Prostitutes too
asleep
under one roof

Bush clover
moon drenched
traveler

Lovely
bush clover
in rain

On the lake drunk
rocking waiting
for fireflies

Soup fish salad
under endless
cherry blossoms

Speaking lips
chill
in the autumn night

Now not even
the morning glory
is my friend

December
what does the man next door
do for a living?

Silkworms
feeble
in the mulberry field

So what if a robber
got in
while I slept

Sweeping the snowy garden
the broom
forgets snow

Squidseller's cry
cuckoo's
which is which?

Chrysanthemums bursting
between stone
seller's stones

Such a sweet odor
in the garden one
shredded shoesole

Bush warbler's droppings
hit
the rice cakes

At the end
of the porch balanced on it
crescent moon

Earth
luminous
buckwheat flowers

Mosquito netting
pale green
in moonlight forever

Stark naked
the Zen monk
sits in the cool evening

Someone tills the field
motionless
at the foot of a hill

An acorn rolls down
the black cold
shingled roof

Wrestler lying in bed
argues about the match
he should have won

A sick old man
slowly sucks
a fishbone

The cloud
can't hold
the moonlit drizzle

Is that orphan
old enough
to chop wood?

The fish slit open
shows it has eaten
a Buddha

Crow on that bare branch
this autumn evening
explain

Bashō and Friends

Bright red maple leaf
a midwife's
right hand!
    Sanboku

One maple leaf
the wind carried
stuck to an icicle
    Itto

The brushwood gate's
polished iron bolt fills its keeper
cold moon on it
    Kikaku

What a backache
in the chilly evening
finally home
    Kyorai

Wish I could stretch out
on the grass and clutch
each branch of the grieving cherry
    Hafu

Zen monk naked
as a worm
loving the breeze
    Zushi Rogan

Her eyebrows beautiful
slender crescents
clear in the luminous moonlight
    Bashō

Motionless man
tills his field
at the foot of the hill
  Kyorai

Sandpapery screech
monkey's white teeth
moon tiptoes on the peak
  Kikaku

Where's that skinny knife
I used for
the last grafting?
  Shiko

Cool paste's still
wet on
a paper lantern
  Issa

Metaphors disgust me
gone with my faith into
the sunlit dried-up field
  Kusatao

Don't be like me
musk melon cut into
two identical halves
  Bashō

What a fate
to be a bamboo shoot
when you're dead
  Bashō

Not a mote of dust
on the white chrysanthemum
soothing my face
        *Bashō**

Hail battering my new hut
still Bashō
like that aging oak
        Bashō

Dusk not dead yet
many nights on the road
and where's October?
        Bashō

Sea slugs
a frozen lump
still wriggling
        Bashō

A toad flops into
the weedy old pond
and nothing
        *Bashō**

*Written two weeks before his death.

Crazy Cloud Ikkyū

who's crying outside my door? ask Kyosie if you don't know
men crazed running after things midnight burns my window blue

green willow red peony journey's finished today
break my staff over my knee burn it in the July snow

mind so calm dream born into this dream of a world
I'll fade first light's dew on a grassblade

for thirty years mere mist mere haze
mist haze sixty years eat Buddha shit die

no wind waves huge who uses this road? all streams converge
but a tiny piece of cloud wipes out empty space

words phrases of the masters monk hating monk like spitting
    blood
Sword Mountain's razor peak's all you know

snow on the ground in the mind is how to do it koan completes
itself head shaved somebody writes poems hungry

picking the cutest whore to fuck this old monk sings as he does it
inspired by her cunt her kisses not a wisp of hellish guilt

meditate write poems you idiots argue about bullshit all day
compassion would have fed the starving monk

knowing you'll die destroys you who can you tell work play want
don't want be blind deaf senseless can't stop any of it

fuck that crow I claim broke open my mind
sitting here thinking of Mori's sweet wet pussy hair

mind never flows each instant the same past present moon
trapped among branches the drinker fondles his cup

no subject-object mystery no form safe life impossible
subject-object fire burning my wooden floor

toiletpaper sutras koans like the shit smeared on them
not one thought while I wipe my ass with my hand

earth corpse heaven corpse gates barriers gone snow a beggar
stops at my door disappears the instant I see him

this cook's amazing one flavor taste the world two spicy fish
gnaw on the head swallow its eyes suck every bone

subject-object koan's beyond me saki dissolves it wind
ruffles the pines and cedars clouds millions of people can't believe it

Zen people fight over Zen poets over poetry snail horns safety
      danger
one knife kills one sword protects that gorgeous woman knows

reckless natural thirty years Ikkyū's Zen is these hundred meat
      flavors
saki gruel twig tea in a white cup

sitting still not there yet laugh at the Śūraṅgama Sutra recite step
      into
a brothel once and it happens

koans stories examples deception arrogance grows
girl in the whorehouse wears gold brocade

clear yesterday stupid today reckless easy acute
dark light trust change shade your eyes stare at the farthest distance

nothing but fucking on my mind drives me nuts wildfire never
destroys it spring breezes grass again

look Zen in sickness years back Pai-chang and his hoe
drunk all night facing hell what about some rice money?

thieves never attack the poor one's money is not the king's this
    virtuous
face the root of disaster millions of silver coins worthless

Zen's going downhill mistakes then mistakes now spring wind
    humming even
without saki poverty's elegance October

these assholes marching down the hall hands folded *gasshō*
    offering incense
flywhisks clapper wooden chair Ikkyū cuts open his anguished
    stomach

incense stink oh how many enlightened masters talk endlessly
    about Zen
how to attain it pious despicable what stinking incense

Zen students have no sense of the truth red purple and gold robes
    veneer
my sincere words like chewing tin I play my music to cows horses

always another barrier behind a barrier rules and examples can't
    break through
exquisite slick delicious lychee given to us

money's more powerful than a god my legs like brittle twigs
song of the griefstricken cuckoo's blood spring in my heart

almost went crazy from training so hard nothing's better
than fishermen's songs sunset rainclouds moon night after night

thirsty you dream of water cold dream about fire
I dream of a girl naked in her bedroom that's who *I* am

nap on the way back from Leaky Road to Never-leaking Road
what Zen bullshit windy rain rainy wind

once I was never here nothing nature never knew me
this Ikkyū corpse rotting like a plum

is as is your question is as is my answer is as is
mind is a doorway without a door

if you think time exists think again the mind
before you the mind after you

sins my ass they don't mean anything like milkweed
on the wind and all my guilt milkweed on the wind

what's evil tell me what have you done that's evil
I ask myself not one stinking illusion left

heard it before all the Zen nuts mouth it breeze moaning in pines
in the black ink image is consciousness no it's the breeze and no
pines

the word *Buddha* is like a barn loaded with cowshit
you don't need to pray to it to smell it

the most powerful truth is that a lie is Buddha lying to himself
and to you each step you take nonsense salvation's nowhere

rain hail snow ice are your face after your dead skull crumbles
into a thousand pieces and a child carries them home

if I hear one more word about seeking the Buddha way
I'll puke I love the chaos passion hypocrisy I contain

I'm asking myself where I'm from and it's as if when I touch my
face
it's nobody from a nameless place with four walls where?

they say it's beautiful but I hate the fact that the cherry blossoms
fall and are gone and have no mind that feels pain

the saucepan's face shaved whiskers on the pebble
each bamboo in the painting singing

these words less meaningful than a dustmote
and what they say is wrong signed Ikkyū

my house is like a paper screen roofless
wind misses it rain can't make it wet

wind howls like a wolf goes silent
not one wolf has ever been seen in this district

clouds up there swirling fleeing gray blue white
it's amazing they can't read a single word

ripples on the unaccumulated water of the undug well
a man without a body hauls water from it

somebody just whispered the word *enlightenment* into my ear
I threw him down and beat his face to a pulp

sure maybe in our deepest nature we're unborn undying
I've heard those notions those terms they make me yawn

crescent full moon no moon empty
dawn and the crescent moon

another Zen idea: the willow the flower have no color
the willow green the flower red you looking at them

anguish grief that's most of what life is
why not love death why not admire ourselves before we were
          born

if I could crush words in my head I would don't give a shit
what they mean nobody's there to read them anyway

we are responsible to express the fact that flowers know nothing
of Zen but blossom in spring drop off scatter become dust and
          nobody asked them to

I helped people I probably even stopped a few from killing
    themselves
but this raging fire called me I can't put out

we're born we die even the great masters
even the cat even the wooden ladle I use for soup

stone Buddhas are stone
I don't want to be stone

even though I know it's noon I don't know what time is
see that mountain in the distance don't know what space is

I won't die I won't go anywhere I'll still be right here
when you come to see me ask me anything

it's a fake all of it seems real I know what an idiot I am
death isn't something that happens to me and you

only the man of mercy sincerity
sees you

I'd love to give you a gift that would make you happy
but in my sect we have nothing

it's exquisite to push my face into a slice of melon eat
the sweet cold flesh wet almost up to my eyes

because I don't think of my body as my body
everywhere I am is the same

no sound no odor that's the mind
any word you use you stole from somebody else

yes it's an echo off the mountain *There is There is*
but not when I'm standing close to it

they say the whole afterlife thing is like numbers written on
    water
I say it's like a stick shoved up my ass

I'm alone and so are you always alone
excruciatingly lonely

what I do is not what I say
it's shameful

lightning evaporates like dew
this ghost of myself

thinking hard about it—me and other people
no difference our minds each other's

don't worry about it dear dear friend I love you
fool sinner condemned saved exactly like me

Daito

Daito's Mind

look
truth's naked radiant flesh
the core shines by itself
no eyes no ears

sky's like a sheet of pure aluminum

nothing
no words for it
desperate to find me
nothing you see

air's fragrant as an elephant fart

or here
is where I am
point to it
just like that

wet grass as tender as a baby's heart

without texts
you are it
just like that
try to see me

road's empty not a cart man or dog on it

through form through sound
in either place
you can't see me
so many years begging

trees leafless like the bones of thought

robes old torn
outside the gates miles of grass
sleeve tatter
chases the moon

hunched on my rainy stoop the old neighborhood cat

roaming everywhere
no footprints of mine are seen
on one tip of a hair I leave the capital
three drum taps I leave Kyushu

car coughs two three times can't start

one glance at the morning star the snow gets even whiter
the look in his eye chills hair and bones
if earth itself hadn't known this instant
old Shakyamuni would never have appeared

sink your teeth into this juicy arm

how boring to sit idly on the floor
not meditating not breaking through
look! horses racing along the Kamo River
that's zazen!

falling asleep's waking to your first face

scoop up water
the moon lies in your hands
toy with a flower
its fragrance soaks your robe

one day I'll lift myself for the last time

please drink this cup of wine
beyond the western outpost
you'll find
no friends

nothing but walls of mist miles ahead of you

full moon in the palace pond a gem
though it's not yet autumn
this very quiet night he's sure the ripples are different
from this alone he'll walk the path deluded

wrought-iron garden chairs like black skeletons

as if it had new eyes
huge Dantaloka Mountain hard as iron
windless night
bamboo grove whispers

a world trying to know itself speaks in unison

I push away from the lamplight
the scroll of half-read texts
only my mind listening
not one master left

this right-hand fist can't bang the sky's aluminum

mind slices a hair
blown against it nothing is cut it cuts itself
nowhere everywhere happens I hear
the emptiness gnash its teeth

taste its black mouth

Hui-neng

Formless Stanza

A real master is like the sun blazing at noon balanced on a
    gold steeple

He teaches one thing: how to realize the essence of mind

He annihilates renegade sects

The great laws can't be split into "sudden" and "gradual"

But some will waken more quickly than others

This method for realizing mind's essence

Cannot be understood by ignorant people

Explain it a million different ways

It boils down to a single principle

Establish the light of wisdom again and again

Wipe the stains from our dreary temple

Wrong views degrade us

Right views keep us clean

When we throw out both we're completely pure

Waking lives in our mind's essence

Seeking it elsewhere is absurd

Deep in our impure mind pure mind exists

Once we're clear mists of hatred illusion lust

Blow away

Once we walk awakening's road

Nothing gets in our way

Constantly watch your own faults

And you can't stray

Leave your path look for salvation another way

And you'll never be where you want to be

Keep on like that to the brink of death

All you'll do is repent repent

Act right and the true way's immediately yours

If you don't try everything to be miraculously aware

You'll rummage in the dark forever

Walk the path sincerely

And you won't see the world's mistakes

Find fault with others

And you are at fault

Ignore other people's faults

Destroy the habit of finding fault

And the source of poison will be gone

When hate or love do not ruffle the mind

You sleep well

If you want to help others awaken

Learn how to use the necessary tools

When the disciple has no doubts

His mind's essence is known

Deepest awareness is here in this world

That's where your waking must be sought

Cut yourself off from this world to attain it

And you'll search for a rabbit's horn

Right views are transcendental

Wrong views are worldly

When all views right or wrong are shed

The core of miraculous waking appears

I give this stanza to the Sudden school

Some call it the Great Ship for sailing existence's fiery sea

Kalpa after kalpa any man any woman may be deluded

But once awake it takes no more than a single instant to attain

Unattainable cloudrock Buddha principle no one can define

Formless Stanza

Idiots call it death

Calm permanent bright as it is

Lunatics call it annihilation

Think of it as not doing a thing

Any idea of what it is is wrong

Fake names invented to help you talk

Only people whose minds are where they are

Not attached not detached

Know its absolute peace

So-called ego things forms voices sounds

Illusions dreams

Wise man butcher the same

Don't affirm don't negate break through

Present future past

Use everything eyes nose hands tongue with no idea

Of what it is to use

Each detail of every separate thing is clear

Catastrophic winds rip mountains apart

Cataclysmic fire burns oceans dry

I'm trying to tell you something I can't say

Like eating mist or chopping your shadow in half

No views that way you'll stand where you are

But listen this is weird—if you don't take what

I say literally you might get a minuscule taste of nirvana!

Formless Stanza

You think that tree's real? It's not.

Forget "real" objects.

Believe objects are real

You're trapped in the *idea* of the reality of objects.

See the mind's essence inside yourself and

You'll know the true mind exists by itself.

Idea after idea filters reality.

Conscious people keep moving,

Inanimate objects stay still.

Forget trying to stay still.

Practice staying still and what you'll get

Is the dumb stillness of a rock or tree.

Oh that butterfly!

Be still and act.

You won't find the oh-so-Buddha-thing by not moving.

Cut this, cut that, know the details of this and that

And the First Principle will run in your blood.

See things this way

And you'll see things as they are.

You who take the impossible road

Try hard, remember

In this school we do not cling to

Birth, death—we talk to anyone about these things

Whether they agree or not.

Be kind to them, make them happy,

But don't argue;

All that does is condemn your mind's essence

To a bitter mundane life.

A Hui-neng Stanza

You think seeds exist in the mind,

Will send up flowers when it rains,

When rain drenches everything,

And they will—

The real truth in all the words,

Beautiful words, ideas, voices

Trying to help, is that insight

You had eating dinner last night,

Picking your nose, that evaporated

On the spot and can't be remembered,

Your unique realization of... Can't say,

Says Hui-neng one more time

Crushing the doctrine-flower

In which hand?

Another Hui-neng Stanza

Friends, I know this is abstract

But I can't find the right words—

To realize nothing can be seen

But still have the idea of invisibility

Is like the sun blocked out

By a fleet of speeding clouds.

To realize nothing can be known

But still think of unknowability

Is like a clear sky maimed by a lightning flash.

When you let those frivolous concepts

Spontaneously fill your mind

You can't see the essence of mind,

Can't even name it,

Can't find the skills to realize it.

Realize for a split-second that random

Concepts like those are as useless as cat-shit

And your own "spiritual light"—horrible term—

Will shine forever, but only if you

Hate the phrase *spiritual light,*

Steal the Buddha's money to buy the Buddha's incense,

Break through to the speech that pictures the experience,

Tell it to others.

Against

What idiots you are

To believe

Sitting and never lying down your whole life

Lying and never sitting your whole death

Will do it—

Why should you punish this

Stinking bag of bones like that

When every instant is its life its death?

Satori

I say nothing I do will do it

Whatever I think I think

Trees wine fish people everything touches me

The word *enlightenment* is a cow turd

Mind Ground

Bungler Hui-neng

Can't stop thinking countless thoughts,

Seeing a flower weeds rainclouds rice a stream

My mind loves them—

I'm here, I'm here,

My lips sewn shut,

My hands frozen fists,

My feet rooted like bamboo.

What can this idiot do?

Issa

Little Wren

for Margot

Look at this world even its
grasses right under my feet
feed us

This cripple has put sandals
on his hands walking in May haze
through the gates of Zenkoji

The beggar's box has
a few coins in it
it begins to rain

Moonlight tints the tubwater
I bathe in its odors
mix with spring beginning

Fleas you too
must feel how long the night is
how lonely

Where are you friend
what moist soft grass is
under your head?

Luminous moon do you
have to rush into
the future too?

Our old dog looks around
as if he hears
the canticles of worms

Insects don't cry we
all have to go
that way

Evening cherry blossoms
fluttering down even where
there's no pond

I define spring like this—
one lone bamboo
a willow twig

I was away forever
and the old village's cherry trees
still flowered

How can the wild turnip
sprout and the skylark warble
at the same time?

Thunderclaps
the peasants cheeping together
like scared birds

She waits on the shore
while twilight widens out over
the darkening tide

Fly on my hat
you're a true citizen
of Edo

That fly wringing his hands and feet
begs you to spare him
begs you for mercy

Such fragile sparrows
opening their beaks at the plum tree
that's how they worship

I can't see my village
but the lark
sings there

Who lived here
before I came
always the violets

Which autumn wind
I'm traveling to
will be hell

Miserably cold
but last year's pine tree
is the same tree

Cricket next door
I heard you
over here

White chrysanthemums
somebody splashed with water
from the washing bowl

This pine I planted
years ago is thicker gnarled
and autumn's ending

Impossible! he asks for nothing
yet he exalts
Buddha

Cuckoo nothing's between us
me and the burweed now
O Bird of Time

And I keep waiting
for you
Bird of Time

Grasshoppers in the chilly breeze
sing
as if you'll never sing again

From up here on the hill
the spacious room
looks cool

Cool breezes
pine tree at the tomb
do we trust the grace that sends them?

He likes the evening too
it seems
that red dragonfly darting by

A world of dew
and even inside that dewdrop
conflicts

January here
but elsewhere
plum already flowering

How lucky to be bitten by
Kazusa's mosquitoes
too

Don't cry little bugs
even the stars up there
part from their lovers

Looms clacking
you insects weaving too
welcome the stars

Pearly dew
in every single one
I see my home

Moon shedding white light
on my face as I sit
a Buddha knees drawn up

A mere cricket
on this frosty night
pierces the frost like a needle

Snow thaws
the whole village
swarming with children

To birds to men
"Take your love now"
these burning fields seem to say

Inside this one
stalk of grass
the cool wind waits

Dews evaporate
seeds of hell are sown again
and again today

Across this human world
a butterfly's existence
wobbles so quickly

Strolling along
even seeing the cherry flowers
you can hear people grumbling

I resign this soul of mine
to a shit-stick
while breezes cool me

Listen to the watery song
of the cuckoo drip
into sleeping ears

Whose is it then
my children
this red red moon?

In this world we
walk on the roof of hell
gazing at flowers

Got it!
to pine trees to the moon
add the virtuous cuckoo

When I'm dead
guard my tomb
grasshopper

Visiting the family
graves
our dog walks ahead of us

How brief a summer
night is say
men in their prime

Crescent moon's
mood is the
cuckoo's

Wild geese be quiet
in this unreal world
everything's the same

A puppy sleeps
with a leaf in its mouth
under the willow

My cottage tucked away
no teeth
but I'm lucky

The minute
the snow has melted
the gnats start arguing

In my house
the fireflies and the mice
get along

January's here
snow flurries
not plum blossoms

Even fleabites on
her skin are beautiful
because she's so young

Got colder
as we learned finally
what the word *parent* means

Right next to each other
a chrysanthemum and cowshit
what a scene!

Trust only trust
and trust again that's how
the dew creates itself

Sparrows
no shitting
on our old quilts!

The insects whine
and chirp each one for itself
just like us

We're leaving now—
flies in our hut
screw to your heart's content

I can sense the breeze
winding and wandering
until it hits my face

Ignoring the dew
that signifies our last day
we bind ourselves to others

The gods are gone
and the black kites go crying crying
about their progress

Cloud veiling
the moon in the wide sky
do you wind up as ashes?

Birds asleep
on the water do you
also wish for luck?

Is burning off the grass
a blessing
or a curse?

You can live here
sparrow
till you've raised your children

One thing you can depend on—
the silkworms on their shelf
will enjoy their meal

Here in the village
how the pale moon
appears in your soup

Am I next
this doomed body of mine
O shrieking crow?

Insects chitter but
the silent emmet
shows us his ass

If things were better flies
we'd ask one more of you
to land on the porridge

Sick
how lovely the river of heaven seen through a
crack in the wall

Windy October
and the scarlet flowers
she loved to pluck

Like a breathing stone
the laudable frog
peers at the mountain

I'm chilled to the heart
the snows of Shinano
know I've been rejected

I love the Buddha
but I'm here too kneeling over my
new lettuce

After all these years
I give myself to you
with not one grain of hesitation

Well here I am
at fifty
spring crazed with its flowers

From now on
it's all pure gain
whatever it is

The motherless fatherless bird
opens its beak again
uselessly

Little wren
is there something you want badly
from the plum tree?

At the end of autumn
it's no small thing
to have been born a man

Like the mosquito larva
I waste my day
and will again tomorrow

Darting out of the nostril of
the huge statue of Buddha
a gray swallow

The dragonfly's eyes
reflect the mountain peaks
miles away

I saw rags
of dissolving fog
through my window

Snail does the
red dawn
make you happy?

Only thorns
grow in my garden
thorns

Seng ts'an

The Not Two

the way is hard   choose choose
don't like or dislike   everything's clear
one hair between them   earth sky
not for not against   the truth is clear
for and against   mind's worst disease
no rest   deep meaning not understood
blank featureless space   just enough
taking rejecting   we think it isn't so
getting entangled   as if it's real
driving away pain   pretending it's unreal
pain vanishes   serene in the One
stop moving to rest   rest will be restless
linger on either   the One is lost
without the One   you're lost forever
get rid of Reality   sink deeper into the Real
clinging to the void   denies what it is
talk about it think about it   it's far away
not liking exhausts you   feuds do nothing
following the One   don't hate the senses
accept the senses   perception is true
the wise do least   folly shackles itself
why prefer anything   why be attached
why thought and thought   who led you there?
ignorance is rest unrest   no love no hate
dream ghost flower in the air   why try to hold it?
is isn't gain loss   bury them forever
eyes open in sleep   can't have bad dreams
not this or that   nothing but truth
the mysterious One   dissolves memories
think of the One   is is is is
no beginning anywhere   no battles left
movement is still   then where is it?
stillness moves   then where is it?

both gone forever   where is the One?
at the final point   with nothing beyond
no rules   all standards gone
all's equal   action is action
doubt's washed away   belief is easy
nothing left over   nothing remembered
don't speak don't think   everything's known
return to the root   the meaning's there
seek the light   you'll lose its source
look into yourself   in a flash
what seems what is the nothing of it all   is yours
don't look for truth   give up your views
is isn't   breed chaos madness
the two exist because of the One   forget the One
no thought   no blame
no blame no truths   no nothing no thoughts
who does what he does   vanishes
nothing is done   when he's gone
who does what he does   does it
space is bright all by itself   no mind does it
no one understands   that amazing sphere
beyond yet here   neither he nor I
The Not Two   is the best term
nothing apart   everything here
this truth was   before all
forever and never   are the same
see it or not   it's everywhere
to trust in the heart   is The Not Two
The Not Two   to trust in the heart
and my serious words   mist
these things   that have no
yesterday   today   tomorrow

Han-shu

Ants

sunlight chickenhead
shivering on the wall's
my dead mother's face

I would never have cut that
white peony but
I hated its beauty

how many billion skulls
smile right now
under my feet?

my ordinary clean hands
held open until
I have to shit

imagining death
somebody else's kind words
finding me

or the inside of a walnut
that cannot see
it's a walnut

like the tip of a needle
death can't be seen but
near it everything seethes

woke with her warm nipple
in my mouth
dogs barking at each other

my koan's a perfect hard-on
that won't go down
no matter how long I fuck

ants on the kitchen countertop
can't see my hand
or feel my lack of pity

even so I'd like to be
someone who lets them eat
they're not dirty

infinitesimal Chekhovs
teach me how
not to brush you away

time's no heavier
than one of you
crawling on my finger

Joshu

Song of the Whole Day

for Bill

Cock cries *kakawakakaa* first hour of the day*
So sad I can barely move but get up anyway
Don't have underpants undershirts
Just ragged cloth that looks like a robe
Underwear has no waist workpants in shreds
Thirty-five pounds of black grime smeared on my head
Just as I am wanting to practice wanting to help
I know finally I'm an idiot
Sun level with the ground second hour of the day
Temple in ruins dead village not worth talking about
Dawn no rice in my gruel
Hopeless at the open window its filthy cracks
Sparrows squabbling no friends anywhere
Sitting alone dry leaves skitter by
Who said leaving home cuts off likes and dislikes?
When I think about it my handkerchief's soaked with tears
Sun rising third hour of the day
Purity is obsessive passions
Having a goal's grinding your face in the dirt
Infinite realm not yet swept
Brows knitted heart rarely content
Rough putting up with wizened old men of the east village
Nobody brings donations here
Untied donkey eats weeds by the steps of my house
Mealtime fourth hour of the day
Aimlessly building a fire checking all sides
No cakes or cookies since last year
Vacantly taste them swallow saliva
Rare that things are together never stop sighing

---

* Traditional Chinese hours are equal to two Western hours.

No good men here or there
Visitors only ask for a cup of tea
Not getting it they stalk off angrily
Midmorning fifth hour of the day
Shave my head can't believe my life's like this
Nothing forced me to be a country priest
Outcast hungry lonely why not die?
A few days back you showed up at my gate
Only wanted writing paper and tea
Sun in the south sixth hour of the day
No problem begging rice and tea
Houses south houses north
Naturally in the north nothing but excuses
Bitter salt sour barley millet-rice paste chard
This should be called only "not refusing what is offered"
A priest's Tao-mind has to be kept solid
Sun going down seventh hour of the day
Not walking in light or shade not knowing the time
Reversing the way things usually seem
Eating my fill no food for days both forgotten
Today my body's exactly like that
No Zen study no arguing about principles
I spread out these torn reeds doze in the sun
Even picturing the future Buddha
Can't beat the sun toasting my back
Late afternoon eighth hour of the day
Someone burning incense bowing
Five old ladies three have goiter
Two have faces black with wrinkles
Rare linseed tea
When silk and barley ripen next year
I pray Rahulaji will teach and heal me
Sundown ninth hour of the day
Nothing to protect except deserted wilderness
A great monk simply flows on no special obligations

Moving from temple to temple is eternity
Words that cut through life's pattern don't come from the
    mouth
Bramble staff for mountain climbing chasing off dogs
Golden darkness tenth hour of the day
Sitting alone in a dark vacant room
No flickering candle
In front of me pure always pitch-black
Not even a bell while passing the day
Only old rats scurrying only my emptiness
What else is needed to have human feelings?
Whatever I think is enlightenment thought
Bedtime eleventh hour of the day
Who can't see the clear moon over the gate?
Back inside sleep's all I regret
Don't need more than the clothes I have on
Head monk Liu ascetic Chang—wonderful!
Talking about goodness with their human lips
Meaningless purse and body hollowed out
So what if my bag's emptied out
If you asked me about it you'd never understand
Death empty purse death empty body
Midnight twelfth hour of the day
This feeling how can it stop even for an instant?
Thinking of all those who left home
A temple priest so many years
Bed made of dirt mat tattered reeds
Old elm-block pillow has no padding
Can't light best incense at the statue of Buddha
I hear an ox shitting in ashes

Buson

One Firefly

for Clair

a dozing priest's white elbow night starting

candle flame touches candle who holds it?

who'll use this little pillow twilight?

two huge doors of the gateway like shadows

yesterday faded and today and today

no underpants the wind blows back my robe cools my behind

sunshower look at the pimples on the frog's back sparkle

clunk of a bell struck carelessly muffled by fog

a woman raves and raves in a boat at noon though it's spring

someone's string broke yesterday his kite's still up there

not one bird sings in the mountain's shadow

plowing! the clouds did not move but they're gone

uguisu its tiny mouth wide open sings while the family eats

holding a butterfly by its wings just the feeling of it the mere
    feeling

a red plum's fallen petals flame on the horse dung

ghost shapes lean with the night toward dawn

shocked by my wrinkled hand plum blossoms what a ravishing
    smell!

in the cold corners of my room flowers glow

petals drunk on darkness on death

find out just how high the cherry blossoms are by standing
    there

rape-flowers a whale passes dims the sea

someone's thrown out a pot it yawns in the parsley patch

bone gatherer you know the violets better than anyone!

five-foot-high iris sticking up from a pond?

heartbreakingly puny beads of dew adorn the caterpillar's
    hairs

night's brief waves throb in an abandoned fire

scoop up that persimmon flower from a shallow well no stars

a wandering priest's coffin hauled past farmers plucking rice
    right now

oh the loneliness in the insane woman's face this summer

what scared the crazy chicken scrambling on my roof?

the road in such a downpour's invisible

it's terrifying this river with no name

sparrows clutching bushes gust after gust

gossiping rice farmers smash the moon against their knees

astonishing how the moon remains while nets and ropes are
    dipped and hauled up through it

a sandal in each hand he crosses the swift river

stonecutter's chisel dipped in clear water to cool

the priest's so happy hanging his mosquito net

one edge of it blows into my face

cool off kick my shadow fluttering in the stream

dawn fish that escaped the cormorants kiss the surface

even the woman who's divorced has to plant rice

sharp sickle chopping reeds fish hear it

a bat dashes by the wife across from my house glances at me

my fist tight in the darkness of my heart one firefly

one two three peony petals toppled on each other

clip the peony mind knows nothing

black ant so clear roams a white peony!

even after it dies the peony's image fills me

hawk-shit splashed all across an iris

a priest can't decide whether to rip up the lotus

lightning wrecked that small house tangled in melon flowers

my feet at the bottom of the hot tub two distorted weird white
    things!

it's a knife through me my dead wife's comb I stepped on in
    our bedroom

cricket crawls up the freezing kettle hook

more loneliness this year even more loneliness more

left my cane somewhere such raw sadness this evening

death soon plenty of time just to enjoy myself

an old friend out of nowhere stands in front of me

must have had a teacher but where where is he!

the moon's even more my lone friend

dropped my pipe in the lake studying the moon

white dew dampens hairs on the hunter's chest

murderer is the water deep where fog hides it?

fish strung up to dry from the eaves of a beach house get cold

lamplight through a crack in someone's door marks the village
    edge

a bottomless pail tumbles walks around in the storm

deer's cold horns pressed close to his body like withered twigs

deer cry out three times nothing nothing nothing

dragonflies quiver on my beloved village's blue walls!

red maples suddenly black join the mountain shadow

young fox why did he cough on a hill covered with bush
    clover?

my indigo towel looks ugly beside morning glories

the candlewick's thinness all there is

melancholy crow in the bleak sky's the voice of human
    anguish

tiptoeing on dishes rats make a bitter noise

ice creeps down edges of the well less and less

hate leaving my blankets to strike the snowy bell

a handsaw sounds like poverty this winter midnight

start the fire with that wooden Buddha!

shrewd birds scouring the onion patch what do you expect?

can't get rid of the lust I feel this old man yearning again

snow on the stirrups of the waiting horse

snow snapping off twigs pierces the night and me

deep snow a priest pauses reading what's carved in stone

frost coats everything but a dandelion by my foot

bones grate against my quilt all night

the mountain stream's a path of solid ice

my teeth clenched to bite off ice from my writing brush

who left that red turnip on the riverbank nearly buried in snow?

the high priest relieves his noble bowels in a desolate field

bare slope sunlight covers a rock instantly weakly

stars this early just before dark console the pale earth

the border guard's hibachi glows ice everywhere else

dog curled up against my door when he twitches dreams
      rattles it

oh to hide in myself sleep never be seen

the charcoal brazier warms the hem of my robe not my heart

the quilt down over my feet? up to my neck?

a roofer's footsteps squash leaves above my bedroom

twisting off plum branches sounds like my creaky elbow

Shen-hui

Explaining It

for Doris

The absolute way's without thought like breath
The basis of it is no action breath
True Emptiness—which means Time exists does not exist
   because everything is time—is the substance
Birds dogs men wonderful cups shoes streams wonderful are
   the function
True Thusness—which means "Is *is*"*—doesn't think cannot
   be known through ideas through thought
The True State never was here—in matter in mind?
No thought except True Thusness—which means this way and
   that
Nothing is here but the True State
Here Not here Here a breath
Walking without legs you get across
IS does not move but it can do anything
Instants of thought don't seek seeking itself doesn't think
No perfect wisdom ever occurs yet physical eye heaven's eye
   wisdom's eye law eye Buddha eye Buddha body Bliss
   body Change body no pure understood breath
Meditate you boil weeds your wisdom dumb as the sky
   whatever you do isn't done by you isn't done this breath
Nature's a fan fanning you substance a wordless iron decree
Being where you are means *hsing* nothing to stop you
Ego Dharma Being Nonbeing holes in a painted nonexistent
   fan like breaths
From the first not a thing is† mind does nothing roads don't
   think

---

* James Joyce, *Finnegans Wake.*

† "[N]either to cling to the notion of a mind, nor to cling to the notion of purity,
 nor to cherish the thought of immovability; for these are not our meditation."
 …"Purity has neither form nor shape, and when you claim an achievement by

Thought? Reflection? Seeking? Attainment? absolutely not
No this no that no coming or going
Grasp it you'll see through past-future our dire mortality now
      in a breath our mortal agony
Then you where you are is breath
Serene silent limitless answers acts
Always empty it works always works it's empty
Works but doesn't exist empty as breath
People creatures are what it is
Real wisdom's when your dead twin suddenly walks up to you
Be clear about this—names quiet emptiness insight knowledge
      action facts—all you
Nothing's in the way everything works like the wind like
      breath
See don't watch yourself see one infinite steel blade cuts
      through "a hair's thickness of an idea that there are
      ordinary men and sages"[‡]
"We wish to know how the conception of death will transform
      a person's entire life, when in order to think its
      uncertainty he or she has to think it in every moment,
      so as to prepare for it"[§]

---

establishing a form to be known as purity, you obstruct your own self-nature,
you are purity-bound." —Hui-neng ("The whole system of Zen discipline may
thus be said to be nothing but a series of attempts to set us absolutely free from
all forms of bondage. Even when we talk of 'seeing into one's self-nature,' this
seeing has also a binding effect on us if it is construed as having something in it
specifically set up; that is, if the seeing is a specific state of consciousness. For
this is the 'binding.'" And "Not to be attached to form means Suchness. What
is meant by Suchness? It means the Unconscious. What is the Unconscious? It is
not to think of being and non-being; it is not to think of good and bad; it is not
to think of having limits or not having limits; it is not to think of measurements
(or of non-measurements); it is not to think of enlightenment, nor is it to think
of being enlightened; it is not to think of Nirvana, nor is it to think of attaining
Nirvana: this is the Unconscious. . . . When the awakened mind is dead, the
conscious illumination vanishes by itself—this is the Unconscious." —from
chapter 7, D.T. Suzuki, *Zen Buddhism*, footnoted "See the *Sayings of Shen-hui*,
section 11.")

[‡]   Wuyeh (Mugo)

[§] Kierkegaard, *Concluding Unscientific Postscript*.

Moonlight on the sea caught by millions of waves sees hears
    realizes knows
Being empty means not being seen breath after breath
Being tranquil means not having been born
Then good evil turmoil calm can't strangle you
Nonbeing isn't non–being breath
Being isn't being breath
Here the asylum of words is razed this is where your face
        floats like a cloudmask where the grass's bright green
        lights up the core of your skull where the "act of
        extinguishing" where nirvana's root is re-seen: "it
        blows" *I I I* smashed by the radiance of a star
No pairs of opposites know your faults**
The bloodstained struggles of birth death—sleeping in the sun
The conscious pressure of who you are—no leaves on the
    branch
Hear yourself breathe
Now you breathe now you're the breath

** From *The Sutra of Hui-neng*, trans. Thomas Cleary.

Ta-hui

No Second Person

Talk about it forever it's wordless
These days people don't get it
Instead they practice this that
Think they've broken through
Don't know the intrinsic isn't what you taste hear see
But the gate of miraculous freedom more subtle than breath
Aware of everything that exists
Pure free
Its light has always shone never gone out
From the first inkling of time until this instant
In you in front of you everywhere
Like a silent rock unchanging
Its great radiance bathing everything
It touches every color
But keeps its singular perfect hue
Like fine silk stretched on a loom light blazes through it
The sophisticated refined don't have it
They don't know what it is
They worship the beauty of forms
But that's like rubbing your eyes
They think they see what they see
They exhaust themselves uselessly
Pounding at it in vain
Pounding at it their way
Millions of years drift away
If you can look back and realize
No second person exists
How did you get here?
Who is looking at whom?
Each act whatever you do

Won't lack a thing
But keep calculating *past future*
You'll still believe this empty fist holds something real
Even when your dead eyes are open

Feng-kuan

Rhino

A fly crawls on his horn.
I stare, minute after minute,
almost an hour,

dazed by his massive silence.
To him I'm not even here,
I'm nothing,

leaning on
the waist-high iron fence.
His haggard lead-hued skin

twitches now and then,
his hulk presses the ground
somewhere in me,

his blank unyielding gaze
holds me so steadily
I forget who I am. He turns

and shits suddenly
while I laugh at the lesson of what
slips out soundlessly and falls

into a neat pile.
His beady passive eyes,
quizzical mouth, mind

of my mind,
his idiotic head
like a fist

faces me again.
He seems not to breathe.
My own breath

slows, disappears,
and a nameless glance—
his, mine—

quivers, hums.
Birdlike he glides
on deft hooves into his

artificial stone cave.
I peer in
and see nothing

but darkness, and hear:
"Keep him inside you
until you know."

Bankei

First Song: 1653

never was   always will be
mind before mind
earth water fire wind
sleep there tonight

you you on fire
burning yourself
attached
to this burning house

search
all the way back
to the womb
can't remember a thing

good bad
ideas
self self
which?

winter's wonderful
bonfire's
ridiculous
in summer

summer breezes
irritate
even before autumn's
over

rich now
you hate the poor
forget when you
had nothing

you saved every dollar
a fiend
watched by famished wraiths
of your self

your whole life
making money
could not pay off
death

clinging wanting
nothing on my mind
that's why I can say
it's all mine

you want someone you loved
now
only because
you never knew her

you can't forget
not to remember
someone you never forgot
who?

looking back
you see it one brief evening
realize   see
everything's a lie

bitter? does this
incredible world of grief hurt?
why wound yourself
brooding on dreams?

all this
is unreal
instead of clutching your head
go and sing

no hands   no eyes
nothing exists
touch see
that's it

your mind
yours
torments you
because you need it

hating hell
loving heaven
torture yourself
in this joyous world

the hating mind
itself is not bad
not not hating
what's bad

good   bad
crumple into a ball
of trash
for the gutter

ideas about
what you *should* do
never existed
I I I

finished
with Buddhism
nothing's
new

enlightenment   really?
"mind"
keep wrestling with yourself
idiot

these days enlightenment
means nothing to me
so I wake up
feeling fine

tired of praying
for salvation   look
those poor beautiful flowers
withering

saunter
along the river
breathe
in   out

die   live
day and night   here
listen   the world's
your hand

Buddhas
are pitiful
all dressed up   dazzled
by brocade robes

enemies
come from your mind
right wrong right wrong
never were

call it this   that
it doesn't exist
except this page
except these wandering phrases

praised   abused
like a block of wood straight through
my head's the universe
can't hide my ugliness my clumsiness

so I just go along
with what is
without anger
without happiness

nothing to see   nothing to know
before after now
call and you'll hear
its heartbreaking silence

Ryōkan

After Ryōkan

Dew drenches the mountain path
it must be freezing there
one last gulp of saki
before I start for home
what about it?

Frogs chortling
in the wasted fields
I pick roses
float them on my wine
just for the hell of it!

Those frogs again
stretching my legs
in my grass hut
what message do the slimy creatures
have for me?

Left my begging bowl
at home but
nobody would steal it
nobody
so sad for my poor bowl

First chill of autumn stuns me
I've been waiting for it
dusk insect cries
rise from the grass
trying to soothe me

Dew clings to the grass
to the whole meadow
did the insects weep all night
helplessly
and leave their tears here?

When I was young
I couldn't care less
how long the winter night was
oil whenever the lamp needed it
alone devouring words

Peonies
at their peak
plump silky sexual blossoms
I can't pick them
I can't stop picking them

Breaking them open
splitting them eating
gobbling picking them apart—what's the "them"?
I'll always suck on them so
delicious never out of my mouth

The pain of life
makes me want to protect
everyone if only my black sleeves
were wider deeper oh this crazed world
I'd put everyone inside

Nobody to talk to about autumn
sorrowful days of nostalgia
I lug a basket of wild dark green
spinach I picked in
twilight on my way home

What should I do
with the nameless color of the water duck's
wings staining the green hills
an unknown bird
from the treetops releasing its aria?

Girls jabbing rice
seedlings into the bed of the paddies
dotting the mountains
their singing drifts up
wordless nobody's voice miles away

Wake in my hut
hail rattles a grove of bamboo
I was asleep before
that noisy ice
blew down

Violets dandelions
mixed together
fill the bowl I beg with
I offer handfuls—don't I?
to billions of Buddhas

When the rains ceased
for a while this autumn
I'd hike the mountain trail
with a bunch of children
the hem of my robe completely soaked

The nights colder and colder
now in November crickets
and all their friends right here
just outside my door say
time to patch your clothes

Plum blossoms we floated
on the wine we drank
have all fallen of course
nobody sees them
nobody picks them up

Yet they appease an old man's heart
and his grief quiets
my close friend
for many many years
gone

My priceless vase is like a friend
not a speck of dust I promise
morning night I'll take care of you
wipe you so you shine
you won't feel lonely ever

Have I really lived
are the years real
did I dream them into the real?
night icy rain flittering on roofs on leaves
can't block it out

I kept asking when
she would come
now she's here
seeing her face
is everything!

Even when this Zen kook
me is still hungry
my shadow lurking
at the bottom of my bowl
seizes the last few grains

Some people
give their lives to others
and here I am
in my pathetic hut just because
I need a little rest

Mist hangs in trees on housetops
long spring days
like a child I play handball
with the children
still alive still alive!

Hakuin

Zazen Song

Each creature all's water and ice
No ice apart from water
Truth's right at your feet not somewhere else
Like thirsty swimmers begging for water
Like a rich man's son lost among poor
Ignorance makes you roam six worlds
Lost in the night of ignorance searching darknesses
Birthdeath how to get free of it?
Sitting's miraculous infinite
Sitting dissolves precepts rules
Walk sitting sleep sitting shit sitting anything you do
Sit once not one sin left
No evil steers you wrong
Look into yourself
Sing the truth of the Self
Of the no-nature self-nature
Beyond all arguments
CauseEffectEffectCause Gate opens then
Path of The Not-Two straight ahead
Your form the form of no-form where? who?
Your thought no-thought
No no-thought no no-form no Not-Two
Leaving returning here's where you are
Singing dancing voice of Truth
You lack nothing now body of Buddha now
Awakening is you

Shitsong

Assholes

Realize this!

Fuck Buddha after Buddha who sees me on the road

They hate me more than I hate them

Every demon with a human face faces without a face despises
    my face
despises my guts despises who I am

I strangle those idiots sitting in silence thumbs up their asses
"being illuminated"

With a silk cord one thick knot in it

I slash the others renegade monks blind bats chewing on
    their shit wisdom

With a knife sharp enough to slice a hair blown against it

This filthy blind old man shaved head gleaming day and night
    under the
sun in moonlight

Piles more dung upon dung upon the dung already harvested
    sculpted
into a Buddha by the rest of you

Deathsong

for Steven Antinoff

Punch your fist mind of a fist through this black wall al-
ways in front of you always the next step you can't
take as you walk into it through it but can't
because it's who you are but can't be do not want
to be nothing but the place where you were are won't
be slam this fist of a fist into the wall that
isn't even here built of the billion nows yous
which when it finally is you finally face it you
pass through like a raw black breath

Stephen Berg is the author of numerous collections of poetry and translations and has been awarded the Frank O'Hara Memorial Prize, a Columbia University Translation Prize, and fellowships from the Guggenheim, Pew, Rockefeller, and Dietrich Foundations, as well as from the National Endowment for the Arts. He has taught at Princeton and Haverford and currently is professor of humanities at the University of the Arts in Philadelphia. He is the founder and co-editor of *The American Poetry Review* and was the editor (with Robert Mezey) of the highly acclaimed *Naked Poetry* anthologies.

Steven Antinoff is an adjunct professor of humanities at the University of the Arts in Philadelphia. He is a distinguished scholar of Zen Buddhism, and for fifteen years lived and studied Zen in monasteries in Japan.

The Chinese character for poetry is made up of two parts: "word" and "temple." It also serves as pressmark for Copper Canyon Press.

Since 1972, Copper Canyon Press has fostered the work of emerging, established, and world-renowned poets for an expanding audience. The Press thrives with the generous patronage of readers, writers, booksellers, librarians, teachers, students, and funders—everyone who shares the belief that poetry is vital to language and living.

Major funding has been provided by:
Anonymous (2)
Beroz Ferrell & The Point, LLC
Lannan Foundation
National Endowment for the Arts
Cynthia Lovelace Sears and Frank Buxton
Washington State Arts Commission

For information and catalogs:
COPPER CANYON PRESS
Post Office Box 271
Port Townsend, Washington 98368
360-385-4925
www.coppercanyonpress.org

The typeface used is Sabon, designed by Jan Tschichold. Display type is Requiem, designed by Hoefler & Frere-Jones. Book design and composition by Phil Kovacevich. Printed on archival-quality Glatfelter Author's Text at McNaughton & Gunn, Inc.